W9-BBI-714

PROMO'S 2 PROFITS

PROMOTIONS FOR YOUR BAR, TAVERN, ENTERTAINMENT BUSINESS, OR SPECIAL EVENT

BY

AARON WRIGHT

EDITED BY PETER MAURER

AVERAGE JOE PUBLISHING
WWW.AVERAGEJOEPUBLISHING.COM

Average Joe Publishing
P.O. Box 2982 Clackamas, Or. 97015

www.averagejoepublishing.com

www.promos2profits.com

www.buildingaprofitablebusinesssystem.com

Contents

Additional Material

Introduction

I purchased my first bar at age 26. I thought that as soon as I got the keys the business would just roll in! Boy was I wrong! Shortly after my friends and family made their obligatory appearance, I began scrambling for business.

As my experience grew from operating my own business and networking with other small business owners, I realized I wasn't alone, there were others needing guidance as well. I began collecting ideas and promo's that helped us generate and maintain better customers, better sales, and ultimately, better profit. I've compiled this Book to share these ideas and strategies in hopes that they will help others explore new ways to profitably operate their business. More important than the ideas within these pages is the creative process that produced them. Recognizing, and encouraging this creative energy, you will be able to mold these ideas to your specific situation, and even create unique, specialized events for you, your employees, and most importantly your customers to enjoy year after year. Good Luck and enjoy the Journey!

—*Aaron Wright*

What Kind of Business are you?

Most small businesses can be divided into one of two categories, a Destination Business (DB) or a Neighborhood Business (NB). To determine which you are, ask yourself these questions: Do your customers travel out of their way to see you? (Destination). Or do they come see you because you are convenient? (Neighborhood). A DB has a different advertising approach, different demographic, and a much different customer cycle (time between visits) than a NB. In a DB your customers have to know what's going on before they get there. They are generally coming in with some friends and for a specific purpose or event, they usually travel in groups, and are generally dressed up, ready for a night out on the town. In contrast a NB's customers come in very regularly and for no apparent reason other than to not go home! In a NB your customers live close, know a majority of the other customers, and don't mind coming in alone. They are usually still in their work clothes and don't mind a messy promotion! Many DB's are a NB the first few hours of the business day, and then turn into a DB in the evening. With the right promoting your NB can be a DB during your slow times. Determining what type of business you are will make it very easy for you to plan the appropriate promo at the appropriate time for maximum results! The Goal…more income, less expense. The key is to know at all times whom you are trying to recruit, where they are, and how you can make them repeat customers.

The first thing I do in any business venture is figure out what it is that I want to accomplish financially. Reviewing the books of the business will give you a lot of useful information, but beware unless you compiled the information yourself; chances are the numbers aren't 100% accurate (I saw a disclaimer on a Profit and loss Statement {P&L} for a business that read, "The information contained herein is deemed reliable but not guaranteed"). Always verify the information you are using to make the best business decisions.

Once you are happy with the information you have in front of you, figure out what you want to earn for yourself. For this example lets assume that you want to make $4,000 per month. Add that to your cost of doing business. Your P&L should show what the business's monthly costs or expenses are (make sure this estimate includes overhead, payroll, cost of goods sold, and a generous misc. amount). Lets also assume that the total costs, including your salary, work out to be $25,000 per month.

Now, decide how many days a week you will be open for business. We'll assume your business will be open 365 days a year, which equals 30.4166 days per month (365 / 12). Next divide total expenses by the number of days the business will be open, which for our example comes out to $821.92. You need at least $821.92 in sales per day to cover operating expenses and your personal income. Remember, this is merely an example and not a substitute for professional tax or accounting services. I'm not the kind of guy that wants to cut it that close, so let's round that daily figure to $1,000 per day.

Now, let's try and figure out how much an average sale is within the business. If you are buying the business from someone else, ask for their credit card transaction history, or if you already own the business, take a look at your credit card transaction history, take the last couple months records and add the total sales up and then divide that by the number of transactions. That will give you a pretty good idea of what your average sale is. Again, for this example, let's guesstimate it at $18.50 per transaction. Divide your total daily sales goal by your average ticket to determine how many transactions you'll need each day to make your goal ($1000/$18.50 = 54). Now we know that we need to see at least 54 transactions a day to make our goal. That would be 378 a week, 1643 per month, and 19,716 a year. Does that mean that we need 19,716 different customers? NO! This just means that we need a CUSTOMER POOL of loyal repeat customers. Depending on your customer cycle you can determine how big your customer pool really needs to be. If you are a NB and your customers stop in 2-3 times a week, your customer pool of regulars could be around 126-189 customers! (126 customers x 3 stopping in three times a week = 378 total weekly transactions x 52 weeks in a year = 19,716 Transactions per year). If you are a DB and your customers stop in only once a month, than you would need a customer pool of at least 378.

One of the businesses I own is a Quick Lube Service center. My customer cycle is once every three months! So I maintain a customer pool of 4000 to maintain my sales goals.

So what does all this mean? It shows that in order for you to stay in business, you have to make sure that at least 126 (378 for a destination bar) of your customers stay happy, and keep coming back! Not liking to cut it close, I would maintain a master list of customers with at least 500 names. These customers are my V.I.P.'s. They are the people that I will periodically send a calendar of events to, coupons, birthday cards, etc.

Read this section again, but this time put your real numbers in place of our example to determine what your customer pool requirement is to maintain the business and lifestyle you desire.

This number will continually fluctuate as your business grows and your needs change. The small business owner should know what their current customer pool requirements are at any given time.

The promotions in this book are designed to create customer loyalty, repeat patronage, as well as broaden and strengthen your customer pool. Let's get started!

Essential Tools

There are three essential tools that will help you achieve your business and financial goals: a Mailing List, a Computer/Printer, and a Desk Calendar.

A Mailing List

The most important tool is the mailing list. Generally direct mail is a costly, somewhat ineffective way of advertising. In this case it is by far your most cost effective advertising tool. Creating a mailing list of your current customers (Master List) is a great way of letting your customer pool know what is going on, and how they can participate. Both the Neighborhood Business and the Destination Business will benefit tremendously from a master list. Here's how you create one…

Neighborhood Business (NB)

There are several ways to build your master list in a NB. Start by contacting a local realtor or real estate title/escrow office and request a pack of mailing labels for the closest 1,000 residents to your business address. I generally start with 10-15 times the seating capacity. Then send them all a postcard with some kind of coupon printed on it. I use the office software on my computer to make all my postcards and print them off at an office supply store on heavy cardstock paper. You can get four to a page. Make sure the coupon is worthwhile. For example:

"Buy one get one free menu item."

This can be anything to entice a new customer to try out your place. One year I sent out a bulk mailer like this and offered a free pumpkin for Halloween! All they had to do was bring the postcard in the bar and pick out the pumpkin they wanted. I sent out 500 postcards and bought 50 pumpkins. The pumpkins made great decorations! 38 postcards came back through the door and they went straight into my master list because they all knew where I was. Of those 38, about 20 became somewhat regular customers and we heard people talking about the free pumpkins for months!

This promo cost me a little over $250, a drop in the bucket compared to what those new customers spend in my place a year!

Free giveaways

We've all seen these, a big jar on the counter offering a free drawing for, Free lunch, Free gym membership, Free movie rental, etc. Come up with something to give away and create an entry form. Make sure to ask for name, address, telephone number, e-mail address, age and birthday on the form. This is a great way to build up your master list.

Destination Business (DB)

It is considerably more difficult to target your market with a random bulk mailing for the DB. My strategy in a DB has been to first try and pinpoint my desired demographic, then get someone's mailing list that has the same demographic.

For example, one bar I had was turning into a music venue for local bands, so I contacted a local musicians newspaper and offered them a lunch party in exchange for their subscription list. I sent out one bulk mailing to everyone on the list with a coupon. For every coupon that came back, I added that person to my master list.

Get the customers that are in your bar to sign up or enter a "contest." Create an entry form with spaces for their name, address, telephone, e-mail, birthday, age, etc. Take their info from the entry form and add it directly to your master list. Sometimes just by having a "Mailing List" at the bar and having a bartender pass it around once in a while will get the trick done.

Ideally you should build your mailing list online, with a click of the mouse you can reach your entire customer base instantaneously using e-mail.

As soon as you start your mailing list and are adding to it, let people know what is happening. Send out a little postcard once a month with your events on it, add a coupon and track it's return rate. I have a policy that if the same customer brings in four or more postcards over a year, I automatically send them a $50 gift card and a personal thank you letter.

You know what your business costs you to run every month, now figure out how much a great customer is worth to you every month? Every year? How many of those great customers do you need to have a really great year? Chances are they are already coming in, if they knew what you were planning for them, they would be in a little more often.

Computer/Printer

A computer/printer and a few inexpensive programs make all the difference! You can create your own postcards and flyers, design and print your own event tickets, birthday and thank you cards, organize your mailing lists, e-mail lists, vendor info, calendar, and much more!

Desk Calendar

A desk calendar is a very important tool in giving you a bird's eye view of all the events or promos you have planned for the month. The bigger the better! It's easy to get focused on a special event and forget about the other 29 days of the month. Pre-planning your month helps maximize your earning potential and organizes your responsibilities. This also makes your monthly postcard/newsletter an easy task to accomplish.

Holidays

Following are a list of holidays that should be on your desk calendar. It's easy to start a calendar by creating events or promo's around nationally recognized holidays. Don't forget to add special local and business specific dates to be celebrated (like your business anniversary). I've included popular promo's I've used in parenthesis for your reference. Good Luck!

January

- New years Day (Bloody Mary Specials all day)
- Martin Luther King Day
- Super Bowl (sometimes in Feb.)
- Jan 16th 1920—national prohibition began (Speakeasy themed night with gangster, flappers, and secret passwords!)

February

- Black History Month
- Lincoln's Birthday

4

- Valentines Day (limo and dinner for two contest/drawing)
- Presidents Day (drink specials and menu items named after dead Presidents)
- George Washington's Birthday
- Groundhog Day (Movie night "Groundhog Day" with Bill Murray)
- Chinese New Year (sometimes in January)
- Mardi Gras (Beads! Beads! Beads!)
- Ash Wednesday (sometimes in March, 7th Wednesday before Easter)

March

- Women's History Month
- St Patrick's Day (hire an Irish musician, poet)
- Daylight Savings Time
- Spring Begins

April

- Poetry Month (poetry contest)
- April Fools Day
- Palm Sunday
- Passover/Good Friday
- Easter
- Earth Day
- Arbor Day

May

- May Day
- Asian Pacific American Heritage Month
- Cinco De Mayo
- Memorial Day
- Armed Forces Day
- Mothers Day

June

- Flag Day
- Fathers Day
- Summer Begins

July

- Independence Day
- Canada Day

August

September

- Hispanic Heritage Month
- Autumn Begins Labor Day
- Back To School (second chance scholarship fund)

October

- Rosh Hashanah
- Columbus Day
- Yom Kippur
- United Nations Day
- Halloween
- Thanksgiving (Canada)

November

- American Indian Heritage Month (Casino Night)
- Election Day
- Veterans Day
- All Saints Day
- Thanksgiving (turkey bowling—frozen turkey and 10 two liter bottles of soda/water)
- Daylight Savings Time ends

December

- Christmas
- Hanukkah
- Dec. 5, 1933 Constitutional Amendment 21 took effect repealing Prohibition (Amendment 18) Yahoo!

Promotions

Most promotions require some advance planning, shopping, organizing or implementation. Take a moment and visualize how the promotion will work in your head, create a very detailed written description of the promo, what you expect, and how, step by step, it will work. Provide a copy to your bar staff so there are no question as to how the promo is to happen. Answering the Who? What? When? Why? How? And Where? questions on paper gives everyone a very clear idea as to what is going on and leaves little room for error. Keep in mind that these ideas are not set in stone, if you feel inspired to alter them to your crowd or circumstance, run with it! Instead of thinking of why something won't work for you, train your mind to pick out the parts that will work and build on that. I have provided lined note pages at the back of the book for you to put these ideas and changes in writing. Good Luck, and remember to always have fun!

Most of the promotions you will find in this book, are promos that can be executed by a bartender, event planner or anyone on site. When the budget was thin I would recruit a regular customer to pull these off in exchange for a bar tab.

As I became more organized, I would place a help wanted ad in the local college paper, asking for a part time event and promotion organizer for a local bar, no experience needed. As the applicants called to set up interviews, I would choose the top 50% of the applicants and share with them the amazing response I got from the ad (this is the perfect college job, you will see a lot of inquiries). Then I would announce a friendly competition to see who would eventually get the job.

I would pair them up into teams, share my promotion material with them (this Book) assign each pair a weekend night (some times the response was so great that I had a different promo team every night for three weeks straight!). I informed them that they would receive 10% of the gross sales for the night of their promotion as compensation for the work they would do (that's what the regular event promo job paid). I let them know that I would be making my decision on who got the job after all the promos ran. I generally hired two or three teams after I saw how creative they got in getting people excited about their event. I placed this ad in the college paper, usually at the beginning and end of the school year.

Prizes and Giveaways

Some of the promos in this book require some kind of prize. The prizes are completely up to you. I explain how to get some of the bigger prizes in the book, but for the littler ones, I am always on the lookout for good bargains. About 75% of all the prizes I use are items I have gotten by trading my gift certificates to other businesses. For example a $20 gift card from my place can get me three movie tickets from the local movie theatre manager, he in turn uses my gift card as an incentive for his employees. The idea here is to limit the cash outlay and maximize the cash income. Whenever you can "trade out" for products or services do it! .

I've also been very happy with giving out date specific gift certificates to my customers for a specific night that I am trying to build up, For example, "Two for one menu items good only Saturday May 14th 2006."

Other great prizes I've given away that cost very little are special drink price bracelets. You can order these at the office supply store and you can print on them with your computer. Whenever you have a little contest, give the winner a $1 off bracelet for the rest of the night. With any luck that will be the deciding factor for them to stay at your place the rest of the night instead of barhopping. Get creative with your prizes, and always keep your demographic in mind.

1.
Jar 'O Junk

Begin with a jar, the biggest one you can find! Fill it with all sorts of non-perishable bar stuff, Bottle caps, Matchbooks, beans, rocks, whatever. Make sure you keep a master list of what is in the Jar and how many of each item. Seal the Jar when you are finished filling it up. The object of the promo is for your Customers to guess how many of a certain thing is in the jar. The closest guess within the time-frame (no more than about two weeks, people tend to get bored and lose interest) wins the prize of your choice. Use a Guess Entry Form complete with the customers name, address, telephone number, e-mail, birthday, and favorite drink! The more info you can collect the better. (start building your master list)

The benefit to you is you now have a mailing list of Customers that know where you are located, have been in your place, and are likely to come back if you give them a good reason i.e. schedule of events. The birthday info is beneficial because you can put them in your birthday club, sending them a gift card for a drink or menu item good for the date of their birthday! Most people don't go anywhere alone on their birthday by getting them into your place on that special day; chances are they will bring friends! Make sure the Jar 'O Junk is sitting somewhere that those "new " customers can see and enter! By having multiple items in your Jar, you can use the same jar over and over.

2.
Table Games

Make a trip to the toy store or local thrift store to stock up on an assortment of table games, Monopoly, chess, checkers, Uno, cribbage etc. Your customers are looking for entertainment, if you have no events planned encourage a friendly table game amongst the other patrons. An alcohol infused game of Monopoly can last several hours!

3.
Birthday Recognition Day

In one of my first bars, I noticed that by the end of the month, business was very slow. I decided to have one birthday celebration for everyone who had a birthday that month. The party was on the 27th of each month. We had a tote filled with birthday decorations that we broke out for a birthday party, or on the 27th! We had frozen cakes on hand, special drink prices for the birthday people and a nice birthday board in the bar listing whose birthday we would be celebrating that month. The customers loved the recognition and it soon grew to one of the busiest days of the month.

4.
Someone Expecting?

This promotion came about when one of our employees and his wife were expecting a baby. I had one of our beer distributors create a banner that read, "John and Suzie are expecting a baby on June 6th, guess the sex, height, weight and time of birth. The closest guess wins!"

I posted a list of prizes, the list continued to grow the closer the due date came. Customers began throwing in gift cards and baby gifts for the family to be. The bar randomly added to the prize pool based on the number of entries on the "guess" sheets. I asked for all their info, name, number, address, e-mail, favorite menu item and birthday. I added their info to my master mail list and to my birthday list. In later promotions I charged $1 per guess with all the money collected going towards a savings bond for the baby.

5.
Gift Card Exchange

During Christmas season everyone gets gift cards that they will never use. I began a gift card exchange day between Christmas and New Years (generally a slow time in our bars). I advertised on the bathroom walls for two weeks prior to Christmas that on a specific day the bar would be having an exchange. All customers had to do was to bring in their unwanted gift cards and the trading would begin at a certain time. As customers mingled, met new people and tried to trade their gift cards for something they might use, I always had a bartender on hand ready to write gift certificates to the bar in exchange for random gift cards. These made great giveaways for future promotions and guaranteed future business for us. Most of the gift cards we issued were day specific, "$25 gift card to be used any Tuesday between Dec. 28th 20. And June 15, 200?." This way I could purposefully build up a slower day of the week.

6.
High Score Contest

Whether you own your video games/ pinball machines or lease them, this promo will work for you. If you don't own the machines or have access to the cash box, you may need to work this out with the owner of the machine beforehand.

This promo is very simple! Just print up a nice looking sign that says, "Whoever has the high score on this machine on _____(whatever date you choose, usually over three to four weeks) wins _____(list a prize that is worth playing for)." We began this promo with a $20 gift card to the bar, then as people began talking about it and coming in to purposefully play we began taking 25% of the games income to fund the next months prize. The highest prize awarded was a $500.00 gift card to the store of their choice!

List on your announcement that if you get the high score go to the bar and tell the bartender, after the bartender verifies the top score, the bartender will get their information on a "High Score" pad kept behind the bar. Don't forget to get their name, address, e-mail, phone number, birthday and favorite menu item!

7.
Name that Mug!

Employees and patrons bring in pictures of themselves when they were babies. Number the pictures and let the customers try and guess who is who. Award prizes for the most correct guesses.

Variations to this promo are...

Use celebrities, show the baby pictures numbered and then post adult pictures labeled alphabetically. Let the customers match the numbers to the alphabet.

A funnier variation to this game is to have several pictures of your regular customers on one side of the wall and on the other have a caricature artist or cartoonist draw "sperm" variations of them, with at least one distinguishing trait for the matching! The sperm caricatures become great customer appreciation gifts to your regulars!

They will be talking about this one for a while!

8.
$ In my tip Jar

I started this when I was bartending and it was great when business was slow! I would have a pretty regular crowd sitting around the bar watching the paint peel. I made a makeshift target out of a piece of paper and cut out a small hole and taped it to the opening of large plastic pitcher. I propped it up against the back bar and we, the customers and I, would take turns trying to make waded up pieces of paper in the jar…I know, real exciting!

I spiced this up when I started putting the "target" on my tip jar and challenging the customers to try and make a waded up $1 bill! I offered to buy their next drink if they made it! Surprisingly almost everyone was up for the challenge. If they made it I would pay for the drink from my tip jar. This was always a profitable way to pass the slower times in the bar!

9.
Open the Box

This promotion started off as a fundraiser but soon became a regular event. What you need is a small wooden or plastic box about the size of a shoebox. I prefer a plastic see through box so everyone knows what's inside. The box must have a padlock on it and a slit in the top to insert money, gift certificates, etc. Start off by having the bar put $15-20 in singles in the box to get things going. Then bring out a ring of 75-100 keys making sure that only one of the keys fits the lock! A locksmith can help you with this; they generally have the dummy keys in their waste bin. You can have fun contests with your patrons to win "time" with the keys and box or just sell "time." When you sell time, you have to be sure and allow everyone who wants to buy time a turn. Explain the rules very clearly. 30 seconds to try and find the right key and open the box to get the money costs $1. The dollar either goes to charity, the bar, or in the top of the box! We started this promo to support local charities, but then began doing it every Saturday night adding the $ collected to the prize! As the prize amount grew, word got out and we saw people coming in just for a chance to open the box!

10.
99 Bottles of Beer on the Wall

You'll need 99 empty, rinsed out beer bottles! Print up different prizes on slips of paper & put them in the bottles (Free drink, menu item, T-shirt, try again, etc). Randomly throughout the night select different people from the audience to choose a bottle and try to win a prize!

A variation of this game is to have several funny or rude comments or "Fortune Cookie" sayings in each of the bottles with just a few prizes in select bottles.

As the night goes on, the number of bottles reduces creating a little excitement because the customers generally do not know what the "grand prize", or the top prize is, so they don't know if it is still in play or not.

11.
Daily/Weekly Drink Specials

This promo came about as a result of hiring bartender after bartender that didn't have the drink knowledge required. I would pull a new drink from a cocktail book each day, trying to match the drink to what was going on in current or local events. Before the shift began I would have the bar manager and the bartenders make the drink together (consistency is very important). Once everyone got it, we would advertise that drink on the Specials board above the bar at a greatly discounted price, and encourage our bartenders to suggest it, sometimes offering little prizes for the bartender that sold the most specials during a shift. At the end of the day the daily specials board was erased, and the special drink for that day was added to the "what's new" board above the bar at normal price. This promotion succeeded in educating our staff to different drinks and to expanding the horizons of our customers resulting in increased sales and more confident servers!

12.
Discount Beer Bracelets

Sell Discount Beer Bracelets for a specific period of time. I began this promotion because I had a really slow period from 7-9pm. So I sold a bracelet for $5 that allowed the wearer to half priced draft beer for that time period. The main goal was to get more patrons in for that time, and it worked, the later crowd began coming in a little earlier and the early crowd started staying a little later increasing sales and tips for both shifts!

I also had a problem of keeping patrons after a specific event, like live music. I had a good neighbor agreement that had us stopping live music at 11pm. To keep people from leaving after the event, I sold beer bracelets good from 11-2am. I charged $6-$10 granting them half priced draft beer and a free appetizer! The free appetizer encouraged more kitchen sales and discouraged large beer consumption. This promotion created a late night crowd coming in after our events specifically for this promotion. Win-Win!

13.
Business Card Scavenger Hunt

For this promotion you will need a larger audience. Once you get everyone's attention, choose two competitors from the audience. On your mark send them out into the audience to collect as many business cards as they can, give them a time limit, and count down loudly. Make sure they know that duplicates will not count! Award the person that collected the most cards a prize, later add the names and addresses of all the cards you collected to your master list, and send them each a "Free Party" letter (See "Free Party" Promo).

Variation...

Set up two or three chairs at the front of the room, on your mark, send them out to the audience to collect a ....Hat! The first one back to their seat earns a point, send them after a number of things getting as creative as your customers will let you, awarding a prize for the most points. Always have a booby prize for the losers.

14.
10% off Your Bill!

This is a simple marketing strategy. Once you have applied for your city license, you probably started getting junk mail for personalized cards, pens, Frisbees etc. Save these ads! The stuff they are selling is of very low quality, but can come in handy!

I ordered 500 cheap ball point pens from one of those companies and had the following message imprinted, "Bring this pen back to the____(your business name and address here) and receive 10% off your total bill!"

I started leaving these pens wherever I went, the bank, the post office, the grocery store… everywhere! This worked very well! I actually came across one of these pens 6 years later. I had sold the business, but called the new owner and asked if the promo was still honored! I was surprised to hear that they still get a handful of those pens returning each month and yes, the offer would be honored! A quick Google search on the internet with the key work "promotional" will get you several companies selling low quality, low cost marketing ideas.

15.
Local Music in the Jukebox

Local musicians will be thrilled to be invited to have a CD of their music available on your jukebox. Even if you don't own your jukebox, the company that does will accommodate your request to install your selections. Be very clear to the musicians that they will not be getting their CD back (too much to keep track of) and that in order to keep it in rotation you expect it to be played at least three times per week (or whatever # you choose). The machine will keep an internal memory of the play list. This request will ensure that they will be bringing family and friends in to your bar to listen to their music on a regular basis!

Require "the band" to organize a kick off party in the bar. They may want to perform a few songs for their fans, friends and family, then play their C.D. several times throughout the night

Finding local musicians is as easy as putting a classified ad in the local college or entertainment paper "Local Musicians wanted, Call the ABC Bar and Grill (###)###-####."

16.
Trivia Night

Trivia night is a general favorite for all types. A box of trivial pursuit questions is all you need. Once your customers are seated with food and drinks in front of them, have your bartender or MC ask questions all at once or a couple at a time allowing music or conversation in between.

Once all the questions for the night have been asked, have the customers swap answer sheets, then give all the correct answers and have them score the sheets. The highest scores win prizes!

Variations would include—

Making each table a team, with team prizes or posting a tough question on the "board" giving everyone with a correct answer a discount or ?

I even did a promotion where I had the trivial pursuit box behind the bar and offered anyone that answered five random questions in a row a free drink, but if they didn't, the drink would cost them $1 more! It was amazing how many people believed they were smarter than they actually were (the extra buck went into my tip jar)!

17.
Random Card Match

You'll need two decks of regular playing cards (not Pinochle cards!!!) one for the bar and one to tape, lacquer or glue to the bottoms of the tables, chairs, barstools or wherever. Randomly, throughout the night, shuffle the bar deck and draw a card in plain view. Have the customers check under their seats or tables or wherever to find the match. Whoever finds the match wins the prize!

This promotion came about because we noticed that customers were getting stagnant in their seats for too long. We needed something to break up long periods of inactivity and to keep the blood flowing. We put the cards under their seats, so every 90 minutes or so they had to get up and check their numbers! It did wonders for their energy levels and longevity!

18.
Bladder Bust

This is by far one of my favorites! Simple, Simple, Simple! First, announce to your crowd that you will be doing a promotion and that the bathrooms will be down for a short time, so go now if you have too! Next, post signs on the bathroom doors explaining the rules—

Bladder Bust!
For the duration of this game, the bathrooms will be taped off!
While they are taped off,
All Draft beer will be half price!!!
(pitchers excluded!)
{or any promotional discount you prefer}
The first person to BREAK THE TAPE ends the game!
And Beer Prices revert to normal!! Good Luck! And Have Fun!!!
Happy Holding!

Make sure to let your customers know that using the parking lot for a bathroom is unacceptable!

I once caught one of my bartenders selling bathroom passes for $5 each, good idea, poor execution.

19.
Balloon Stomp

This promo is a little silly, but it is a lot of fun! First you'll need a few things to get started, a bunch of rubber bands and balloons (9-10" balloons and regular office sized rubber bands). Each customer will need one balloon and one rubber band. Have your guests blow up their balloon, the bigger the better, and tie it off. Then have them tie it to the rubber band and have them slip the rubber band over their left foot at the ankle.

You should have a room full of people with a balloon at their left ankle. On your mark, instruct them to stay in the Play Area (the dance floor or bar area, whatever you choose) their goal is to protect their balloon and pop other balloons at the same time. Once their balloon has been popped, they can no longer pop any one's balloon and must sit out for the rest of the game. The last balloon standing wins a prize.

This game gets crazy at first and them turns hilarious towards the end! Call a time out if it looks like things are getting too serious and make light of the situation. Change the rules if you have to to keep a jovial mood.

Suggestions include—

- A blindfold
- No hands

Each contestant has to hold two full glasses of water while attempting to pop their opponents balloon.

The more risqué groups such as bachelorette parties, use blown up condoms instead of balloons. Try attaching them to their wrists instead of feet. Biting allowed! (make sure someone has a camera!).

20.
FREE Raffle

I had a problem with customers leaving too early. So we came up with this promotion and it worked very well. We bought raffle tickets from our local office supply store (double tickets, one for the customer and one for the bar). We would give the customer tickets with every purchase beginning at a certain time, say…7pm. Then every hour on the hour we would draw a ticket and give away a prize saving the best, biggest prize for just before closing. The customers that had been there since 7pm would have several tickets thus increasing their chances to win the best prize(s). I found that the best "Big" prizes for just before closing were local sports tickets, NBA, NHL, etc.

I generally dedicated 10% of my daily ring out to promotions, so if I had a $1,000 night, I would spend, or giveaway approximately $100 in cash or prizes.

On particularly busy nights we would do a 50/50 raffle, where people could buy a raffle ticket for $1 (these would be a different color from the free raffle tickets). $.50 of the money would go into a prize pool for the one winning ticket at the end of the night and $.50 of the money went to the bar.

21.
Customer Parties!

Your regular customers (anyone that is on your master mailing list) is a potential goldmine for your business. A good portion of your day should be keeping these people happy. One way to do that is to give them preferential treatment or V.I.P. status in your place. Obviously knowing them by name helps, but with the information you have on them you can do so much more! If you know when their Birthday is, why not have a little party? Do you know when their Anniversary is? Retirement date?

All the contests that I have ask for their birth date. We have a tote of birthday decorations on hand and birthday cakes in the freezer. When one of our "regular" customers has a birthday coming up, I send them a nice birthday card generated on my computer with a gift certificate good on their birthday for a drink and the menu item of their choice. Since most people generally don't spend their birthday alone we have a pretty good chance of them bringing in their friends for a "quick" drink.

I take it a step further if it is a customer I know by name. I send them a birthday card and the gift certificate and also 15-20 business cards printed up (on our business computer) as invitations for them to hand out to their friends announcing that ABC Bar and Grill is having a birthday celebration for our friend on their birthday from 7pm–9pm.

We also post the proposed party in the bar for the other regulars to see. The total cost is less than $2.00 (not counting the gift certificate) if the customer has a problem with it they will let us know, if not, than I will see a few new faces on party day! I generally defrost a B-day cake, break out the Happy Birthday Decorations, get a few balloons and pass out a store-bought card for everyone to sign. We sing the song and then other customers buy the B-day person drinks all night long. Everyone wins!

22.
Tip Chips

Tip chips are designed to accomplish two goals, first to encourage generous tipping, and second to invite customers from a busy night to a less busy night. Here's how they work—

Create the tip chips, you can use wooden nickels, buttons, or simply a business card. If you use wooden chips or the like, glue it to a business card with a full explanation, "Good for____(two for one, $1 off a menu item, a FREE drink, ect.) compliments of ____.(space for the bartender to enter his/her name) Good on____(enter a specific date that you are trying to encourage business)."

Then distribute these cards/chips to your bar staff and let them know that they are to hand them out to their best customers as a Thank You gift from them and the bar. Explain to the staff that the purpose of this promotion is to show appreciation, introduce that customer to another night at the bar, and to encourage customer gratuities.

23.
Silent Auction

The silent auction promotion is a great way to raise money for charity, sending a customers child to camp, Christmas families, ect. It really compliments other promos. It is something for your customers to do while something else is going on. For example, I would run a Silent Auction along with live music, or Karaoke. Here's how it works—

You will need a group of prizes.

Make them crowd specific (if you are having a sports event, make the prizes sports related, etc)

Try and get most of the prizes donated, or trade your gift certificates for them.

Either display the prize at the bar or attach a picture of it on a piece of paper. If you had to pay for it, start the min bid for what you paid. If not, start it at a crazy low bid to encourage bidders. Print Name, Tele #, Address, Bid Amount across the top of the page just under the description or picture of the prize. Make sure there are plenty of pencils or pens, a pen on a string attached to the wall near the bidding form works well!

Next, post the bidding sheets throughout the room and instruct your customers to take a look at the item, and bid a little more than the previous bid if they are interested, winning bidder will be the highest bid amount at a certain time (be sure to specify what time it will end).

The most successful silent auctions I held were during bachelor and bachelorette parties, with a portion of the proceeds going to the Bride and Groom.

If the prizes are good enough, people really don't care where the money goes!! We've been really fortunate putting prize packages together from various donated things, like a dinner and movie package, or bowling and pizza. Anytime you can throw in a hotel room at a nice place the bidding goes a little crazy.

You'll find that at the end of the night, when money is collected and prizes are awarded, most people pack up and leave. Try offering everyone that placed a bid whether they won or not a special drink or menu price. You have a good chance of keeping them a little longer! As a "Thank You" for participating we offered half price drinks for the first thirty minutes following the auction. That kept about half the people in their seats for a little longer.

24.
Bachelor/Bachelorette Parties

Your space may or may not be the ideal place for a bachelor/bachelorette party, but it is surely the perfect place for the before and after party! By having a party package suited to your space, you are sure to get some increased business. When this promo was created, I had a space that would seat only about fifty people with a pool table and pinball machines. It wasn't really set up to host private groups and events, so what I did is work with a local limo company and came up with a before and after package where, for a set fee, I would arrange for the party to all meet at the bar, have a few drinks, get into a limo, to go wherever they chose for a few hours and then bring them back to the bar where an appetizer platter would be waiting for them.

By working out this plan in advance with the limo company, having a planned pick up and drop off time, they could book more than one event in the same Limo and give us better prices. By offering this program, customers didn't have to worry about their car and we got the before and after business that we wouldn't have had otherwise.

25.
Limo Promotions

This promo started out as "Formal Night." I rented a limo for the entire evening from 8pm-3am (half hour after closing). I advertised for weeks before our event. For $50 per couple, they would get a limo ride from their home, to the club, dinner for two, special drink prices all night, live DJ after10pm and a local photographer taking pictures. The evening ended with a limo ride home when they were ready!

The limo company gave us a great deal because I let them hand out their business cards to all the customers, some of the smaller limo companies were happy to trade out their services for gift cards. The photographer came in for free and tried to sell his pictures (the deal was that he gave the bar the pictures that he developed that he couldn't sell).

Over the years I tweaked this promo around a special comedy night, 21st birthday, poetry readings, live music, etc. I have even sold this type of party to our business neighbors having them pay for the limo and entertainment for a special party for their employees.

If reservations are slow to this event I would start giving away gift certificates made on our computer good for limo transportation to and from the bar on that night. Which turned out to be a great way to build up a slower night and have something of "value" to give away on the busier nights.

26.
Pack Your Bags!

This promo requires a little pre-planning. The bar/host/promoter puts together a great little overnight getaway (we are close to the coast, so I would rent a room for the night at a beachside hotel, throw in a $30 gas gift card, a bottle of champagne and two champagne glasses) then we would advertise the overnight getaway a few weeks prior to the event. The customers that wanted to go had to show up to the bar with their bags packed! We would do some other promotion to determine the winner, a raffle, contest, or silly relay depending on the crowd. The winner would leave right away because the room reservation was for that night!

The most successful event I did was a weekend trip to Reno! The total cost to us was a little under $300. I had a taxi ready to take the winners to the airport right after the Karaoke contest. I held this event over five weekends each weekend having a contest with the winner competing in week five for the trip. All five finalists showed up with their bags packed and friends in tow for support on the final night. It was a great success!

27.
Vendor Appreciation

The people/businesses you do business with are a great resource for you to ask for a little return patronage! Create a list of everyone that you do business with, from your local mail carrier to your food and beverage vendors, don't leave anyone out!

Next divide this list in groups of twelve (months per year), add the names of each group to your promotion calendar. January group one, February group two, and so on. Prior to the month starting, send the owner or manager of the vendor for that month a Thank You note. Your card should read something like this,

"As a token of our appreciation for the great service you provide, we've chosen the month of _____ to be vendor appreciation month,

offering you and all your employees _____(insert your promo-
tion here buy one get one free lunch menu, 50% off any single item, etc).
In order for you or your staff to take advantage of this promo simply
identify yourself (a paycheck stub or company badge will suffice) to
our staff prior to placing you're order. In addition to this month long
promo for you and your company, we would like to host your next com-
pany party, Employee Appreciation dinner, or social hour! Please give
_____a call at (__)_____ and we'll work out the details! Again,
Thank you for the great job you do. Please forward this on to the rest of
your staff, we look forward to seeing you all soon!"

Send this letter to the companies that you've chosen for the month
at least a week before the month starts. Make sure you post a small di-
rectory of the companies that will to receive the promo prices for your
staff's reference. Make sure your staff understands this promotion!

28.
Neighborhood Garage Sale

This event became a yearly event for our neighborhood tavern. It started out as an opportunity for us to get rid of some outdated bar stuff,
then some of the regulars started adding a few things here and there,
it quickly became a free for all and demanded a little organization. The
final result was a two day event where people brought their unwanted
but re-usable stuff to the bar. I posted flyers announcing the neighborhood junk sale and advertised in local papers and on our community
board (see Community Board promo). The money collected went to

the annual picnic. We had a local thrift store stop by at the end of the second day to pick up whatever didn't sell. Business was always good during the sale!

29.
Scavenger Hunt

This promo is a great way to stock up on silly yet needed future give-aways, prizes, and props for future promotions. It also gets a new and adventurous group of people in your door!

Place an ad on a free local web service, like www.craigslist.com or use your e-mail list to get the word out. Explain that you are having a scavenger hunt for the following items (carefully list the scavenger hunt items and quantities). Then offer the first 15 people through the door with these items prizes. This can be whatever you choose, as-suming that whoever is going to see and respond to the ad has never been in your business before make sure the prize is something that would encourage them to come in with friends to use it.

For example—

1. A karaoke party for you and ten of your friends.
2. 4 tickets to_____ (any upcoming event you are planning).

This promotion is designed to attract new customers and to stock-pile things you need for future events, like rubber bands, balloons, fishing line, a mannequin, etc. We would also do scavenger hunts for canned food to give to needy families, toys for needy kids and clothes and blankets for the homeless. It was a fun way to get our community working together.

30.
Hat/T-Shirt Promo

The goal of this promo is to get your apparel out there and let your customers do some advertising for you. I had our logo embroidered on baseball hats and t-shirts, then we offered an instant $ .25 off on every drink purchase if you were wearing your logo clothes in the bar (Or 10% off your final bill).

At first I thought this was a little hokie, but then the regulars started figuring out how long it would take them to have their hat or shirt paid for by their savings! It worked out well and we were able to charge a little more for the clothes!

Variations of this promotion—

Have a specific t-shirt made advertising a specific event.

Make the t-shirt the event ticket, everyone wearing the shirt on event day gets _____(whatever promotion you see fit).

I did this once and sold the shirts for $75 giving the wearer free admission (we had a band) all they could eat spaghetti, and all the cheap beer we could legally serve them! The event was a fundraiser for a regular customer going through an uninsured surgery. This event was a fun way to get everyone involved in helping a neighbor out without creating the awkwardness of asking for donations. We sold over 150 shirts and overall raised over $4,000 for the family! Needless to say everyone had a great time, and our customer was overwhelmed! Stay creative and stay profitable!

Currently there is a company in Portland Or. That will silkscreen small quantities of shirts with custom artwork very inexpensively. Check them out at www.modified.com

31.
Get Paid to Advertise

As mentioned earlier, a bulk of my advertising budget goes into direct mail. I target my audience and send them 4x6 postcards. The postcards are simply 8 1/2 X 11 sheets of heavy cardstock paper cut into fourths. There are plenty of very inexpensive software programs that allow you to create your own postcards. To minimize my advertising expense I sell a small business card size space on my postcard to a local business.

For example, if my target audience is the 22-46 year old that lives within 5 miles of my bar. I approach several small business in my area that have that same target audience; lawyers, realtors, massage therapists, financial advisors, mortgage brokers, mechanics, pizza delivery, video stores, insurance agents, the list goes on. I use the front side of my postcard for my promotions while on the back the right half is for the addressee and postage, the top left corner is for my bar name, address and telephone number, and the bottom left corner is the space I sell. I always encourage the person advertising to make their ad a coupon so they can see the result when the customer returns the coupon to them.

A mailing of 100 postcards costs me a total of $30. I generally send out about 500-1000 per month. I charge $150 for a business card sized ad per 500 postcards, making my mailings free! Some advertisers will pay much more creating a little profit.

Many of my advertisers have contacted me! They saw my postcard with other local business on it and wanted to know how they could get such targeted advertising. WinWin!!

32.
Coloring Contest

Ok, here's another idea that I thought was hokie, but I tried it anyway, and it paid off big! I started putting baskets of crayons at random tables and had a blank 8 1/2 X 11 piece of paper with this brief instruction printed on the top.

"Create a picture of the bar, bartender, or owner. Entries will be posted and voted on by customers. Winner gets $25 gift certificate. Make sure your name address, e-mail and phone number are on back, no info, no entry."

I thought I was asking for trouble, expecting a bunch of lowbrow jokes at my expense, but I was pleasantly surprised. There were a few not so flattering pictures, but all in all they were pretty good. Half the fun was laughing at ourselves! The buzz this created was amazing. People I hadn't seen in a while started coming back in just to vote and see all the goofy pictures!

Cheap, easy and created a new energy!

I did this same promotion at a pizza place I had for a new logo, it was great, I got a lot of new ideas, and a new logo all for $25!

33.
Group Meetings

Are you experiencing a lull in the weekday afternoon? Try offering your space as a meeting space for a local group or organization. Posting a simple ad on a free local web site like <u>www.craigslist.com</u>, or contacting your local chamber of commerce may give you some leads. Neighborhood associations, small business organizations, lodges and community support groups are always looking for a change of scenery. Using the universal law of like attracts like, putting bodies in your place will most definitely attract others.

Offer to cater for the group at a discounted rate for a trial period. Soft drinks, muffins and sandwiches go a long way!

34.
League Play

League play events almost always guarantee an expected outcome at an expected time. Use the entertainment your business already has available; pool table, pinball, shuffleboard, video games, dart-board, etc.

Finding the appropriate league organizers is pretty easy. Start by posting a sign up sheet on your community board or near the restrooms. On the bottom of the sheet ask anyone interested in being the team captain to contact you (on the number listed). When they contact you ask them what experience they have and if they know the area representative. Most "captain- types" already know who to contact or how to contact them. This is your opportunity to delegate, their first duty as team captain is to find out what you have to do as a team to get involved. If they truly have no clue, have them call around to other bars, do some research and report back to you.

In addition to entertaining your own customers, league play is an excellent opportunity for you to show your competitors' customers what you have to offer.

35.
Challenge the Competition

Sponsoring softball, mush ball, bowling, ect. team is a great way to show customer appreciation. However, it seldom works out to the bar's advantage. Instead, get a small group of your customers together to challenge one of your local competitors to a one on one game. By working with your competitor, you can plan enough in advance to organize practices and strategy meetings to truly maximize profits.

Advertise the challenge throughout your bar, and get the competition to go halves on a trophy for the winning bar. Spring for a multi-plaque trophy so you can repeat the challenge every year with the winning team displaying the trophy between match ups. To really spice things up, put a little wager on the challenge. A money wager is always lost on the patrons and creates a weird tone, but "Servant for the day," or a losing team car wash for the winning team always promises great stories and long-lived memories!

Here's how I made this work for me. I challenged the neighboring bar to a five person-bowling match. We set the game for two months in the future. I got my booze distributors to print up a few banners for advertisements. I contacted the local bowling alley and promised to pack their bar on the night of the challenge in exchange for free bowling on the event night, shoe rental for all the players and four free practice sessions prior to the event for each team (always be aware of the bottom line). They also let us hang one of our banners at the bowling alley announcing the challenge and the date.

Then I posted a sign up sheet in the bar announcing the challenge. Having only five spots on the team, I had to hold tryouts. I had over 30 people try out for the team. We used one of my free practice sessions to hold tryouts on a Sunday morning (our slowest time of the week). We all spent so much money in the bar of the bowling alley that day that the owner offered us a stack of free game coupons to give away to promote our challenge. Our team was set with 5 players and 27 subs!

I organized a number of strategy meetings in my bar and scheduled the remaining practice sessions. A few of the local papers caught on to what we were doing and wrote a few lighthearted stories building momentum.

When it came to Challenge day, our overall sales had increased 32% and we had an amazing 120 people show up for the match. Most people watched and drank, but some of them bowled, which made the bowling alley owner even happier! The trophy was delivered to the alley. We had a great time, and everyone left looking forward to the next match up! The after-party at the bar was the second highest revenue-generating day I had. A very successful promo!

36.
Vendor Promo Teams

Check with all your distributors. Many times they offer seasonal promo teams to promote a specific event or product. The Coors Lite team used to come out and set up casino type games and give out prizes.

The Bud Light swimsuit ladies were always a big hit!!!

Check with the local Cigarette distributors and call your local radio stations. Let them know who you are and find out what they have to offer you.

Generally there is no cost to you, and you can book them far enough in advance that you can get some advertising out.

37.
You've Got Beer!

This promo is simple, and it is surprisingly popular. All you need is a big chalkboard or dry erase board. Across the top write, "You've got BEER!" Buy your buddy a drink and bar staff will write his/her name on the board, and then wipe it off when they get it!

The system I saw was very easy, they had two different prices for draft beer, and three different prices for booze (bottles, wine, and top shelf excluded). They used colored pour caps for the different prices; well = blue, call = red, top shelf = black. So they used that color dry pen on the board to write the recipient's name, that way any bartender would know based on the color what was paid for, and for whom. For draft beer, orange = domestic, brown = import. Very easy!

38.
Community Board

A community board within your establishment is essential! Not only is it a place where you can announce upcoming events, it allows your customers to post announcements of their own, such as a car for sale, roommate wanted, etc. Giving them a sense of ownership and increased responsibility, which translates into customer loyalty.

Bordering the community board with bar photos, and event snapshots is always a conversation starter.

A corkboard with lots of pushpins is all you need, placement near the bathrooms or a payphone is optimal.

39.
You've Won!

Break out your mailing list! This idea can work for anything, but I am going to illustrate how it works using a Karaoke party as the prize. First select about 40-50 names from your mailing list. Next, compose a letter on your business letterhead—

Date

Dear Customer,

You've won a Free Karaoke Party for you and 10 guests! Your group will receive:

- *Reserved V.I.P seating!*

- *Discount Drink Bracelets!*
- *Souvenir group photo!*
- *Complimentary appetizer platter!*

Give me a call today and we'll set up your party!!!
(Insert your name and telephone # here)
Sincerely,
(Your signature)

P.S. If your unable to claim this prize you may give it away to a friend or family member, however if we do not hear back within ten days from the date on top of this letter, we will choose another winner. Congratulations! We appreciate your business and look forward seeing you soon!!!

I came up with this promo after hiring a Karaoke DJ that promised a great crowd that didn't show. Some of my regulars enjoyed the change of pace, but I couldn't gamble on another low sales night. So I came up with this. By sending out 50 letters, I received 22 back and was able to spread them out over four weekends. With this crowd alone I know I would have profitable nights. Naturally friends brought friends, so it turned out to be a very good month! I booked 5 parties per night for a total of 50 people. My seat capacity was 100 and I was counting on regulars and DJ advertising. It worked out well and in subsequent events I booked only 4 parties per night and saw the same turnout.

The V.I.P. seating was a sign that read "reserved" somewhere near the stage. When the party arrived they were given bracelets good for $1 off their drink purchases all night. The souvenir photo was a Polaroid taped inside a "Night Out" greeting card made on our business computer. A staff member would take the photo after the group had a few drinks, or if they were all singing on stage. Often one photo would not be enough, we charged $5 for additional photo's. The complimentary appetizer platter was served early in the evening. It serves 5, so this almost always encouraged additional food sales.

40.
Name in Lights

Materials needed: A string or two of Outdoor Christmas Lights (the big ones!)

String the lights on the ceiling or wall in your bar, in plain sight of your bar staff and customers, Plug them in. you're customers pay a small fee to put their name on a lit bulb. Whoever has their name on the last bulb burning (usually takes several months) wins the prize! You determine the prize.

I saw this promo at a local hotspot, the lights sold quickly, the clientele was college aged and I think they just liked seeing their name on the wall. The bar offered a gift certificate to the winner and donated all the collected money to charity. The interesting thing was how often they would stop in to check on their light. Great for repeat business!!

41.
Local Business/ Vendor Appreciation

Compose a list of all the companies that you do business with. Vendors, Suppliers, Services, don't leave anyone out no matter how big or small their business, Then compose a form letter with your company letterhead…

Dear ???　　　　　*Date*
To thank you for your continued excellent service, we would like to host an appreciation Cocktail/Social hour for you and your employees.

The service we've come to expect from you and you're exceptional staff has been an ideal model for us in our commitment to serve our customers. Please call me personally & let me know if Wednesday, May 6th works for you, or if Thursday, May 14 from 6-7pm would work better. We look forward to seeing you and thanking you in person!

Sincerely,

(Your name and contact info)

Check your local laws to determine if you can offer complimentary champagne or cocktails, or just a nice appetizer. A Thank You card and Personal greeting by the Owner/Manager will easily get their party started.

The goal of this promo, is to get a group of people in your place that normally would not come in. Once they are there, it is up to you and your staff to get them to come back again and again. Offering the group special drink or menu pricing on certain days is one way to keep them coming back. As the owner or manager, you should get to know the manager or owner of local companies and suggest their holiday parties and employee appreciation events be held at your place.

Generally in this promo I will tell the organizer that I will provide a round of drinks or an appetizer platter and ask what they would like. This opens the conversation to them picking up the tab for their employees for a certain time period or for a certain dollar amount. I generally offer them a pretty good deal to get their ongoing business. It is smart to let them know that you want to show them a good time so they will consider you for their company outings and parties. I will also hit them up before they leave for another event. A follow up call a week or so after almost always ends with a reservation.

42.
Bake-Off

Tired of cooking? Try a Bake Off! Announce the Bake-Off three to four weeks in advance. Post a flyer on your community board or throughout your bar that explains the bake-off. Have copies of this flyer for customers to take home.

Anyone who wants to be involved prepares their favorite dish (enough for 10 people to sample). They pay a small entrance fee and bring in their dish. You provide a long banquet table for all the dishes, small pieces of paper for voting, and organize the prizes. Each dish is displayed along with a number. Entrants and other customers buy a paper plate and utensils for a nominal fee (usually I give each entrant a free plate).

Each person gets one vote. At the end of the buffet add up the votes and award prizes/cash.

Variations include; main entrée, desserts, BBQ, themed food (Irish, German, Italian).

43.
Pinball/video Game Giveaway

You'll need to buy a used pinball or video game in good working condition. Bring it in your bar and set the price to play to $.50 or $1, depending on your crowd. Place signs on and around the machine letting people know what's going on and why the inflated cost to play. "Whoever has the High score on ____(date, far enough into the future that you make a profit) Wins the Machine!!"

One of the essential parts of this promotion is to get a game that the customers will want to play and ultimately take home. By contacting the company that provides your other coin operated devices and explaining this promo, they may be able to hook you up with an appropriate used machine that they no longer use. Try to work out a deal to pay for the machine when the promo ends.

Word of mouth will create all the advertisement you need. The ideal length of this promotion is 4-6 months.

Depending on the age of the machine and it's scoring capabilities, a log may be needed. If this is the case keep the log behind the bar and instruct players/bar staff that only witnessed high scores will be recorded, so if a player has the high score he/she must call over an employee on duty to verify and enter the score into the log.

It is also important to collect all the players' information, name, number address etc. and add it to your mailing list. Continually update the Leader status on flyers throughout the bar and on your community board.

44.
Bar Olympics

What does your bar have to offer? Video games? Pool tables? Pinball? Darts? Shuffleboard? Big Screen?

Make a list of what you have available for your customers to do. Review your list and choose 3-5 activities. These will become your Olympic events. Come up with a time limit, or an objective for each event. For example, 15 minutes on the pinball machine, record the "athletes" score after 15 minutes. Another event might be to time the athlete on the pool table, how long does it take them to break the balls and make them all in.

Ideas for events can be pretty creative. For example, double the dart throwing line, one-armed pool, coffee can stilts or an obstacle course through the bar. Bring in a putter and make your own putt-putt course. *

Once you've outlined all your events, post the events and a sign up sheet. Allow a few weeks between the posting and the actual event. On event day have a poster board ready with all the events and "athletes" names. Record their scores next to their names as they complete them. You can have prizes for each event and then a bronze, silver and gold for overall winners (your local party supply store has plastic medals reasonably priced). I've seen some places charge an entrance fee and have some pretty great prizes, others have used bar type prizes. Make sure you take lots of pictures!

Be creative and have fun!!

* Blindfold darts was an unfortunate event
* Broomstick pool was a great laugh

45.
Midnight Delight

I first saw this promotion at a local mom and pop bar. The bartender shouted out, "Midnight Delight in 5 minutes." I must have looked as puzzled as I felt so the bartender offered to let me in on what was happening. She explained that there were raffle tickets all over the bar, under chairs, taped to the tables, candles, walls, pool table, etc. As she said this I noticed one on the side of the ashtray in front of me. She went on to say that the bar adds $10 a day to "the pot" and at midnight every night the bartender on duty has a patron pull a ticket from the big jar of tickets. If someone is sitting on or near the number called, they get the pot!

As soon as she finished her explanation she grabbed the jar, filled with at least 500 tickets and asked if I wanted to do the honors. As I was digging for the lucky ticket, she announced that there was $280 in the kitty to be won. I pulled out the ticket; she called the number, waited ten seconds, and said, "Time. No winners tonight, try again tomorrow."

About five minutes later someone found the number. It was as if the regulars were trying to memorize the number and it's whereabouts. A couple of other patrons at the bar started telling stories of the highest pot they'd seen. Then others told stories of when they'd won and what they did with the money. This was definitely keeping them all in the bar until midnight each night!

46.
Chicken Sh#t Bingo!

You'll need a medium sized cage and a live chicken. On the bottom of the cage, create a grid with 50-100 squares. The squares should be 2-3 square inches each. If you are borrowing the cage and chicken, you can make a cardboard cutout for the bottom of the cage with the grid on it. Number each box 1- ? (however many squares). Use a separate piece of paper to list 1-? (number of squares on the sheet). Go around to your customers and sell the squares for as little or as much as you think you can get. A customer can buy as many squares as they want. Once all the squares are sold place the chicken in the cage.

Then just wait. Assign someone to keep an eye on the cage.

Wherever the chicken relieves itself determines the winner! It's up to you to decide how much of the collected money goes to the prize. The most successful times I ran this promo it was split where 50% went to the winner and 50% went for a charity or event like a wedding party, breast cancer, bar's adopt a family, etc. Some customers like to argue about whose number got hit the most, and some even try to get a second place booby prize. (for second place we've always offered the opportunity to clean the cage!!)

47.
Live Music/ Dj

Hiring a band or DJ every weekend can really affect the bottom line. Especially, if they don't come with a following of there own.

To eliminate the risk in live entertainment, I get the Band/DJ to do the legwork. I will print up 500-1000 business cards with the name of the band(logo, if they have one), the date and time they are scheduled, the name and address of the bar, and a cover charge. I lay it all out on the card to look like an event ticket. Then I give about half of the tickets to the band itself to hand out/sell to their family, friends and followers. They get to keep this money (if any) as their fee for playing. I distribute half of what I have left to my bar staff. They also get to keep what they sell. I usually give the staff that is working the night of the event a majority of the tickets. I really don't care if they sell the tickets or just give them away, as long as people show up for the event!

Then I create a flyer promoting the event and send the flyer along with 10 "event tickets" to as many neighboring businesses as I have tickets for. Included is a note inviting them and their employees to enjoy the show free of charge! I keep a list of the businesses that I send these tickets to, making sure I don't send the same company free tickets every week. I try and space out the free stuff about every six weeks.

On event night, I require the band to provide a door person to collect the tickets and I allow them to charge a cover to the non ticket holders for the first hour. Since we are not a venue, I don't want to alienate my regular customers. They all know the cover is dropped after the first hour.

By putting a price on the ticket, I am creating value for the event. The band makes money from selling tickets, my bartenders will make some extra money by selling tickets, the neighboring businesses will score some points with their employees just for passing along the tickets, and the bar will profit from the food and beverage sales on event night. WinWin!

48.
Free Legal Advice

I sent out a post card that advertised—

FREE LEGAL ADVICE
MONDAY, MAY 6TH
FROM 6:30-8:00PM

(This happens to be my slowest time of the week.)

"Joe Smith, a new attorney to the neighborhood will be set up in the dining room offering free legal advice to all who are in need!"

"Joe Smith" was a young man that had just passed the state bar exam and was starting his own law practice just down from the bar. He had wandered in after signing his new lease agreement for a celebratory drink. I was working that day, and as a good bartender would, I started up a conversation with the new guy. We talked about his plans and how he was going to promote his new venture. Like many new business owners he had no idea how to promote.

Seeing an opportunity for us both, I suggested he offer free consultations to my customers in hopes that a few of them may have a real need for his expertise. He was excited about getting some new prospects. So I printed the postcard mentioned above and sent it out to my mailing list of repeat customers. I also made up a flyer and posted it in the bathrooms.

May 6th rolled around, Joe showed up a little early. He set up in the dining room, moving things around to have a little privacy. Before we were finished setting up, about 45 minutes before it was time, people started showing up with tattered file folders and determined looks on their faces. They organized themselves along the bar making sure newcomers knew where the line ended.

It turned out to be a great night for business. Our lawyer friend was able to make several appointments for paid legal work, and became a loyal customer. We ran the free legal clinic on the first Monday of each month for about six months. After that we didn't have to worry about Monday night business and Joe was pretty busy himself.

A few years later I sold that bar and used Joe during the transaction as my attorney. The whole process took about six weeks and I was expecting a final attorney bill of more that $2000, but instead of a bill I got a thank you note for helping him build his business!

This promotion is very easy to set up. Look around your neighborhood. Lawyers, like all businesses, need new customers almost continuously. Make up your plan and approach them. If they say no, ask them if they know of anyone just starting out that would benefit from this idea. This is a WinWin promotion. What you are offering is very valuable to the right person.

49.
Speakers/Guests

In one of my bars it seemed no matter what I did I couldn't get the Sunday business going. I was able to build nicely on the other days of the week, but Sunday was a loser and bringing down my averages for the rest of the week! Then, almost as a joke, a friend of mine who was a mortgage broker, asked if he could hold a two hour home buying class in the bar on Sunday.

He had made arrangements at a local hotel in their conference room, but somehow his reservation was lost and the space was no longer available. He was in need of a space large enough for about 50 people. Oddly enough that was about how big my dining room was. Happy to help, I agreed.

The class went well. About 43 people showed up and they had little booklets they followed as my buddy spoke. We sold 27 lunches and, after telling the story of the hotel reservation mix up, he encouraged everyone to order a drink or two. The relaxed atmosphere promoted open discussion. The two-hour class turned into a four-hour discussion. My buddy later told me that this was the most successful class he'd put on so far.

Best of all people saw cars in our parking lot and stopped in to see what was happening, customers beget customers. We began hosting the class every other Sunday and our Sunday business began to build. Soon enough word got out that we offered a free meeting place on Sunday afternoon and my Sunday problem disappeared.

Some of the groups that have used the space...

- Group Guitar lessons
- Realtors
- Pampered chef parties, candlelight, and naughty girl parties. (Surprisingly these have been some of the most profitable groups, usually a bunch of women out of the house having a few drinks, lunch, and a few laughs. The consultants are very grateful for the alcohol-enhanced sales!)
- Soccer team meetings
- AARP meetings
- Local business association meetings
- Neighborhood association meetings
- Union meetings
- This list is only limited by your imagination

50.
Bartender/Employee Incentives

Your employees are your greatest asset and your worst liability! Good employees make the difference between bankruptcy and prosperity. Finding honest, upbeat and motivated employees is only half the battle. Keeping them happy, positive, and on task is the real challenge. Here are a few promotions that keep them involved, interested and excited to work for you while increasing sales at the same time.

Business card promotion—

The idea of this promotion is to have your bartenders hand out the bar's business card with their name on it and a special offer on the back. We would actually have new cards made up with the bartenders name printed on the card, then order a rubber stamp with the special offer so we could stamp the back of the card. The employees would hand out the cards for a certain period of time (we used six weeks). The bar would put a certain dollar amount in a "kitty" for every card that came back and when the promotion period was over the winner (the one who had the most cards returned) would win 70% of the "kitty" second place received 20% and third got 10%. We placed a few rules on our contest such as:

- You can not give out the cards before a customer pays their bill, but you can give them one for their next visit (honor system)
- when a card comes in you must reflect the discount on their final bill and staple it to the bar copy of their ticket.

Our first stab at this promotion was for a new item on our menu, an appetizer platter. We were trying to attract larger groups of five or more, so we created a large appetizer platter with a combination of the foods we already offered. We had a rubber stamp offering 50% off the appetizer platter. This was a pretty aggressive offer, our goal was to at least break even while the contest was in play, giving the customer a chance to try out the new menu item at a great price and to create demand for the product in the future at regular price.

We set up the contest for a six-week period. We printed 500 business cards for each employee, and 1000 with a space to write a name for new employees or if someone ran out. They all had the bar's logo, address, phone number and we had a little fun giving each bartender a title such as, "Alcohol Specialist," "Bartender to the Stars," "Mixologist," etc.

We held an employee meeting explaining the contest and that we would put $3 for every card received into the prize pool or "kitty." When the contest was over whoever had the most cards redeemed would receive 70% of the prize pool, 20% for second place, and 10% for third. It took about four days before we started seeing the cards come back. By the 7th day of the promotion we were getting 10-15 cards redeemed per day.

At the end of the contest we had sold almost 800 appetizer platters, and the great part was that only 663 were discounted with a card! So we had a prize pool of almost $2000. Our first place winner received a little more than $1300. We held an employee meeting and very publicly awarded the winner his $1300… in $20 bills!

Everyone was very excited for the next contest. I had a few regulars who halfheartedly complained that they were not involved in the contest, claiming that they were "Chairholders" of the bar instead of "Shareholders." Knowing that the whole idea is to get the business cards out to as many people as possible and build customer loyalty, we happily included the regulars in the next contest granting them their "Chairholder" title and name on our business cards!

In our third month after the first contest, appetizer platter sales at regular price leveled off at around 300 per month. Accomplishing our goal of attracting larger crowds our overall sales increased an average of 13%.

51.
Employee Intern Nights

Assign each of your interested employees a night or day of the week that they get to promote. Help them come up with a theme or an idea, give them a budget and incentive, then let them loose.

This idea has helped out tremendously when employees start showing signs of disinterest in their work. Everyone in the world thinks they can do your job better than you. Give them the chance.

As far as incentives go, I generally will figure out the average sales of the "event" night, for example if the employee has the first Monday of the month as their intern night, I will look back at the previous months first Mondays and come up with an average sales figure, then I will offer that employee 10% of actual sales over and above that number as an incentive to plan, and organize the event

This is one of my favorite management tools, because it accomplishes several beneficial objectives.

It gives the disgruntled employee a chance to walk in your shoes to see how challenging your job is. If they are disgruntled, chances are high that you have been a little stale in your promotions, so it gives you a much-needed break. This gives the employee and manager/owner an opportunity to work together creatively instead of reactively. Everybody wins!

Some employees really step up to this challenge, while others fizzle out quickly. Overall, the experience is very beneficial to the business, the customers, and the general working environment.

52.
Pop Culture / Current Events

This promotion is very specific to your business slow periods. First take a look at your sales and determine what days or nights you want to build up.

Then take a look at what's happening in your community at those times.

Next, create a like event or promotion in your place. For example, one of our slowest nights of the week was Thursday night it was like a ghost town! No one wanted to work because it was so slow.

I began asking around and learned that my regulars mostly spent their time at home watching the Thursday night line-up on NBC. This is when the television show "Friends" was on the air and a mega hit. The more I thought about it, the more I realized that I could not compete with the show, so I decided to use our big screen for a "Friends" party every Thursday night.

At the time our big screen was at the other end of the dance floor (that wasn't being used on Thursday night) so I picked up a couple nice used sofa's from the local classified and started advertising within the bar for "Friend's" night, I tried to make the dance floor look a little like the opening of the show with the sofa's and a coffee table. For the first night I offered Free appetizers and drink specials. I wired the T.V. to the stereo system and played the audio of the show throughout the bar.

The first night was an O.K. turnout, about twelve people showed up. By the second week, the word was out! We had couples and small groups, generally the ladies sat on the couches and watched the show and the guys played pool and drank.

The old saying, "If you can't beat 'em, join 'em," definitely applies here. If you are having a hard time building your business on a certain day or night, take a look around and make the necessary changes. The people are out there, find out where they are and what they are doing and then make it easy for them to do it in your place.

53.
BINGO!

When I was younger I thought that Bingo was just for the blue hairs (old ladies…sorry, no offense intended) and Church groups. Then I went into this little bar near a college campus and I had the most fun ever playing BINGO What made it so much fun here were the prizes they gave away! Bear in mind that this place was near a college campus that catered to the college crowd. The games ranged from Straight Line, to "X," to Four Corners, etc. Prizes included packages of toilet paper, a case of Top Ramen noodles, boxes of condoms and so on.

The last game they played that afternoon was a rollover game. Everyone could only play one card and the bingo caller called out only ten numbers. If there was no winner than a prize was added to the laundry basket of goofy prizes that you were playing for. The laundry basket of prizes grew each week until someone won the rollover jackpot, then a new laundry basket started.

I think the trick to having so much fun was making the prizes specific to your demographic. To find the bingo supplies and a variety of trinket give-a ways try orientaltrading.com

54.
Golf Tournament

Golf tournaments are always a sure fire way to promote business. Organizing the tournament is usually the most challenging part. I have found that local golf courses will actually do most of the work. Find one near you that already has a plan and schedule, all you have to do is set the date, advertise within your bar, set up the prizes, trophies and after party. To get the most out of the planned tournament I also negotiate reduced greens fees for a couple practice days (either 9 holes or driving range times) and plan a great party after each practice at the bar.

As for prizes, talk to your suppliers and get them to sponsor a hole or a trophy. Call local real estate agents get them to sponsor a prize in trade for a little advertising on your flyer. Try all your local mortgage brokers, massage therapists, insurance agents, the pizza place down the street, ect.

You can always get the golf course hosting your tournament to give gift certificates for you to use as prizes. I had a good friend, who is a realtor, sponsor a $1000 prize for a hole-in-one. He brings a cooler of beer, a lawn chair and a book on tournament day and sits near the green on the hole he sponsors. The chances of someone getting the hole in one are pretty slim, but he makes sure everyone in the tournament leaves the green with the story of a chance to win $1000, a cold beer and, his business card! For him the risk is worth the reward, and you can bet people are talking about him when the subject of golf, or real estate comes up.

Take lots of pictures, put them on a disc and have a slide show a few weeks after the event to give out the "best and worst of" awards based on the photos taken. A copy of the photo disc is an economical award for these folks.

55.
Friday The 13th

Friday the 13th is the perfect excuse to throw a great themed party! First off, set the tone. Here are some ideas—

- Play horror flicks all day, have a specialty drink with a themed name, like "The Black Cat"
- Create as many superstitions as you can within your bar
- Display a broken mirror behind the bar (you can create this effect with an erasable grease pencil for existing mirrors in restrooms and throughout the bar)—Set up a ladder at the front entrance that your customers have to walk under to get in (use a big enough ladder as to not make it unsafe or a fire hazard).

Get your customers involved, find out what their superstitions are before the party and work with them, make it a masquerade party, or a murder mystery party. The possibilities are endless! Friday the 13th is a great excuse to do something other than a regular Friday night. Remember, one of the reasons you got into this business was to have fun! So do it!!

There are other calendar specific dates that are also great excuses for above and beyond parties. Take a moment and look through your calendar right now and start making plans. If you don't, chances are pretty good that your competition will.

56.
Airplane Toss

This promo came about when I was a bartender and bored out of my mind. I had only a handful of customers and they were a bored as well, but loyal!

During a random conversation, I started folding a paper airplane. I felt pretty confident with my finished product and proposed a little wager with a nearby customer.

"I'll bet you $1 I can hit that neon on the other end of the bar." The contest was on and within half hour we had six patrons any myself creating our most flight worthy creations. As the afternoon progressed a series of rules were voted in.

- No dipping any part of the plane in your beer
- No using coaster pieces to add weight
- No crumpling your plane and throwing it like a baseball.

It was a very democratic rules committee. Each of us got the opportunity to create and pilot our aircraft. We unanimously decided that we needed a rematch with some better materials than the bar offered. We all agreed to build our planes out of a single piece of cardstock paper with no use of tape, staples or any other materials. We were allowed to decorate with pen or pencil, crayons or markers (this was getting serious). We set the date of the re-match for the following Tuesday.

Thinking this was just a silly little testosterone competition, I didn't give it too much thought, until the next night I worked, the word was out, other customers wanted to compete as well. The contest was for distance. We decided the winner would receive a beer from each loser. To gauge the competition, I started a sign up sheet with the rules stated on it and posted it between the bathrooms. By Tuesday night we had 35 entries but only 28 had showed up. This had brought in 20 more people than the last Tuesday. We had the contest, everyone had a great time, my tip jar was very, very happy! We continued this on for the next four or five Tuesdays until we kind of all lost interest in it, but it sure changed the mood of Tuesday night!

This can also work using the beer coasters that the suppliers provide. Make sure your rules are set before the match. For instance, each player gets ten coasters, players take turns at the same target, and loser cleans up!

57.
Male Review

This type of event takes some planning. In my area, we have a number of strip clubs, but only a few places that offer male dancers. If the story is the same where you're from, then a ladies night with male dancers will probably work for you too.

At the time my bar was a neighborhood bar that attracted mostly couples in there thirties and forties. So I set up my male review night on a Friday night, I called around to the escort companies and found a Chip'n'Dale like company that had male dancers. My wife went to their office and picked the dancers for the show (tough job for her!). Based on what the dancers were going to cost, I figured out how much I needed to charge for a cover, I conservatively figured I would be at about 75% capacity. I figured that if I could recover the fee to the dancers with the cover charge, I would do well with the bar sales. I started advertising within the bar that the ladies night would have a male review from 8pm-midnight, no men allowed until after midnight (I didn't want any jealous husbands, or neighbors telling on their wives).

I really had no idea what to expect. As the excitement grew, I printed up pre-sale tickets on my office computer at $10 each and advertised that it would cost $15 at the door. Unlike men, women travel in groups, so I was pleased to have sold more than enough tickets to recover my expenses. The night was a great success; the husbands and boyfriends were very supportive and came in at midnight to hear the G-rated version of what went down from their wives.

This party was a record breaker for the bar, but something else happened that I hadn't expected. The female customers felt a much bigger part of the bar and started coming in much more often with their husbands and boyfriends. All of a sudden they felt included and became more involved. We began having a ladies themed night about every six weeks, no men allowed until midnight, that was a must as far as the ladies were concerned!

58.
Charitable Events

One of my biggest concerns as the small bar owner is that the population at large has the impression that you are a billionaire so they hit you up for every charity contribution, fundraiser, or nonprofit group known to man. Saying no is a part of being in business, but when your regular customers ask for your support, it's a little harder to turn them away.

Sometimes you have to say no for one reason or another and sometimes you have to just whip out the checkbook. Most times when you want to say yes but the money is not available or you've already given too much there is another option: sponsor the event.

Mrs. Jones tells you that Mrs. Smith, a good customer of yours, has just been diagnosed with cancer. She is taking up a collection and wants you to pitch in. You can't really afford to whip out the checkbook, instead you offer to hold a fundraiser in the bar.

Organize an event with Mrs. Smith in mind

- A spaghetti dinner
- Have a raffle
- Get things donated from around the neighborhood
- Throw in a couple date specific gift certificates from your place for nights that you are trying to build up.
- Create a Win/Win situation.

Make it clear that all the proceeds from the spaghetti dinner and raffle go directly to Mrs. Smith and her family. Your alcohol sales should be above average enough to cover any expenses incurred, and you will be helping raise much more money than you would have been expected to contribute.

This type of event is perfect for the local softball, mushball, pool league, dart league, send my kid to Europe or whatever! The trick to see these opportunities is to be creative, not reactive. Every situation offers an opportunity. It is your place to recognize the opportunity that best suits the situation. Remember—"Everybody wins, or nobody plays."

59.
Date Night

The date night promo can be used anytime of year. I will usually pull it out in late summer or towards the end of January for Valentines Day. Simply stated, it's a raffle for a nice evening out. First I organize a date specific package (weeknights are best because it's usually less expensive). One way it works well is if you organize a limo, dinner for two at a nice restaurant, and a nice room at a local hotel.

I try to trade gift certificates for the items I include in the package. Planning the night out on a weekday is usually very beneficial to all of these companies because the weekday is generally their slow time. They use my gift certificates for employee incentives, give-aways or other promotions. If I have done a good job, the date night I am raffling off will have cost me nothing except some gift certificates. My gift certificates are in increments of $20. My thinking is I want the businesses to give them to more than one person effectively exposing my business to as many people as possible.

Create a flyer to hang on your community board explaining the Promo, be sure to include the date and times. Add the sentence " YOU MUST BE PRESENT TO WIN" to insure a larger crowd.

In my neck of the woods, it's illegal for me to sell the raffle tickets. Check with your local laws to see if you can sell the tickets for profit or not. If not, give away free raffle tickets with the purchase of every pitcher of beer, appetizer, ect. I'll do this for a week to ten days leading up to the drawing date.

In the meantime I will be collecting prizes. Suppliers often donate miscellaneous stuff, other patrons that own neighboring businesses donate stuff, create date specific gift certificates for your place for nights you are trying to promote. On the night of the drawing pull three or four tickets every hour starting at about 8pm. First give away the smaller prizes, then the larger ones. Make it last long enough so the Date Night drawing is held about an hour before closing time.

60.
Christmas Lights

This promo is very fun! I'll rent a school bus and driver for about 4 hours for a date in December. I start advertising tickets for the bus the first week in November. The bus will hold 40 passengers comfortably. I take the price of the bus and double it for a little profit margin, and then I divide that number by 20 to get my price for 20 tickets for the bus.

I now have 20 tickets left over, which I give out throughout the next few weeks as promotional prizes.

Usually the tickets sell out quickly so we start doing fun(ny) contests in the bar on selected nights for the remaining tickets.

On the event night everyone meets at the bar, we have a few drinks. Depending on the bus driver, sometimes we make a pit stop at the grocery store and he/she lets us bring a few drinks on board, then we tour the Christmas lights in the neighborhood. When our time is up, we head back to the bar and we enjoy the rest of our evening. Good times had by all!

When I started this promo I rented a limo, but the groups got too big. More people is much more fun!

61.
11 Week Karaoke/Singing Contest

This promo is an eleven-week commitment. First off, create a flyer explaining—

Beginning on Friday ____ (fill in a date) we will start our $1000 karaoke contest.

To qualify you must show up on Friday night and sign up before 7pm.

The entrance fee is $5 and due to time we will only let the first 10 people enter.

The winner of this Fridays contest will be determined by audience applause, in the event the judges feel there is a tie, you will be asked to sing another song for the tiebreaker.

The winner will be granted a spot in the final round, singing for $1000 total prize money, $750 first place, $150 second place, and $100 for third.

The final round will be held on Friday ____ (11th week).

Runners up may come back next week as one finalist will be chosen for the next ten weeks for the final round.

The final round will be decided by written vote, all customers on that night will be charged a $2 cover charge and given a ballot upon entrance.

Votes will be collected at the end of the last performance, the top three contestants will be asked to perform a second song, and the audience will then cast their final written vote.

Prize money will be awarded immediately following the vote count.

Ok. Those are the rules. By charging each contestant a $5 entrance fee, we raised $500 in entrance fees. The $2 cover charge for the final competition was designed to recover the other $500 for the total prize money. By making this contest audience decided, we had ten weeks of several different people bringing in all their friends to vote for them. This in turn made for really great sales nights without tapping all of our regular customers.

Then, on the 11th week, we had the ten finalists for their final shot at First Place. They had a lot to gain by getting everyone they knew into the bar to vote for them. The reason I took the top three and had them re-sing was to make it a little more talent based and not so popularity based. By knocking out seven competitors, their friends had to vote for the person they thought was the best of the remaining three.

For the ten weeks leading up to the finals, we had an average of 120 people in a 1500 sq ft bar, for the final round we had over 400! It was wall to wall! Needless to say, the entrance fees and cover charge paid for all the contest related expenses, and the bar sales were off the charts! Everybody wins!!

Leading up to this contest we offered several $100 karaoke contests on the same premise, except we did it all in one night, we limited it to the first 12 contestants bringing in $60 in entrance fees and charged a $1 cover. Eliminating the bottom seven contestants (by applause, or lack thereof) and having the top three sing-off

In the beginning of this book, I talk about building your customer list. When I ran the 11-week contest, we had each contestant fill out an entrance form collecting their name, address, telephone number, birthday, and favorite drink. We had a total of 83 different contestants, I added them to my birthday list, Master list, and immediately sent them a thank you letter offering a special cocktail/karaoke party for them and ten of their friends. I was able to book 34 parties from that mailing.

62.
Battle of the Bands

Bands are always a lot of fun. If you are like most bars you get tons of calls from local bands asking if they can play for you. Some of them will play for free which is always a bonus, but I got tired of letting the free ones play only to have no-one show up to hear them, so I developed the Battle of the Bands. Here's how it worked for me...

I blocked out every Saturday night for an eleven-week period on my events calendar, I placed an ad in a local musicians newspaper and contacted all the bands that had contacted me in the last six months.

Before long I had 15 bands that wanted to participate. I chose the first ten that committed and kept the other five on hand. I assigned each of the ten bands to one of the Saturday nights. Leaving the last Saturday night for the finals. I asked each band to play at least three forty five minute sets with a twenty minute break in between. All but one band chose to play more. I made $1 off drink coupons good only on Saturday nights during the ten-week period. I had them printed in ten different colors and gave each band about 1000 cards in their respective color. Each band would be assigned a color and receive one point for every coupon that came through the door. On performance night, they would receive one point for every person that came in and paid a $3 cover. They would also receive one point for every dollar in bar sales that came into the bar that night. The top three bands (having the most points) at the end of the ten weeks got asked to play the finals (the 11th week). They were to set up in half an hour play a 30 minute set, and tear down in half an hour.

It got a little crazy, but it all went off pretty well. The cover charge for the final week was $5 and the audience had a ballot to vote. I had a local radio DJ, and a friend that owns a music venue in the city come by as judges that could override the audience. My plan was to award all the cover money to the three bands with a 70-20-10 split. I knew that in order to get their interest in the beginning I had to offer a guarantee that would be appropriate for them. First I decided to purchase 10 hours of studio time in a local studio. Then I promised that 20 t-shirts would be printed with the winning bands logo. And I guaranteed $100 second place. The promotion worked better than I expected and I was able to not only give the prizes I promised, but first place got an additional $200, second place got 5 hours of studio time, 20 t-shirts, and the $100 promised, and third got 5 hrs of studio time and $50.

(The studio gave me a great deal on the additional 10 hours when I told them what it was for.)

All the bands involved made it on my master mailing list.

63.
Turkey Bowl

You'll need a frozen turkey (or chicken), ten 2-liter pop bottles, and a long narrow area; like a dance floor. A carpeted area works well to. The turkey kind of rolls more than slides.

This is a great thanksgiving time promo. Once you set up the pop bottles like bowling pins, your customers can't help but form a crowd. Be prepared! Make sure you have a sign up sheet handy; everyone will want to go first. Make up the rules as you go. If you have some cheesy prizes lying around, give them away for a split pick up, or a strike. Bowling alleys give away tons of free game cards as a loss leader. Stop by your local bowling alley and ask for some prizes.

If you empty the pop bottles, the strikes are fast and furious, it's best to keep them full, or refill them with water.

I would usually award the sad, thawing bird to the winner of the game or the most animated player, and the full (shaken) pop bottles to the others, as the game lost its luster. A ten frame game lasts a little too long, a five frame game is just about perfect! You'll be amazed at how many questions you'll have to answer in the coming weeks by customers who missed the fun. The important thing is that they will be talking about it for weeks to come.

64.
Broomstick Pool Tournament

Yes, you've played pool with a pool stick, but have you played with a broomstick?

This is a holiday favorite. It seems that people are more open to crazy ideas around the holidays.

The structure of this tournament is the same as any other.

Everyone pays an entrance fee.

You can set it up as a single elimination or a double elimination.

Make sure you have plenty of broomsticks on hand (the thrift store is a perfect source).

I have always made my entrance fee about the same as the price for a drink and then pay out the top three 70-20-10 split.

A fun variation to this, is to make it a timed competition. Time each contestant breaking and clearing the table in order, or not.

65.
Wet T-shirt/Boxer Contest

The wet t-shirt contest has always been a crowd pleaser for the guys. It's easy to get a cover charge for this promo. The trick is to get the prize money attractive enough to get quality participants.

I have never been too fond of the traditional wet t-shirt contest. I always felt a little left out; I wanted to be the guy with the bucket of water! So I came up with my own version of the wet t-shirt/ boxer contest.

The premise is the same. Wait until your crowd is ready for some fun, and then announce the contest and organize your "models" make sure to have plenty of cotton t-shirts/boxers on hand, then when everyone is ready, ask the audience if there is anyone that would like to be in charge of the water? At this point the crowd goes a little crazy, everyone is volunteering themselves or their buddy. Immediately whip out your big bucket of Squirt guns! Big guns, little guns, all kinds of water guns! Announce that all the money goes to the winner and let the "Contestants" sell the guns for you $1, $2, $5, whatever they can get

Mixing up the "models" is fun for all! When all the guns are out, get the "models" on-stage and count down for fun. The winner is determined by applause. Collect all the water guns before the applause vote. Your staff can be re-filling the guns during the vote for the next round. Have Fun!!

66.
Party Games

Blindfold Team Relay
- Divide into teams
- One team member is blindfolded from each team—The teams are instructed to guide their blind member around the bar and to the finish line by yelling directions across the room.
- First to make it wins!

Obstacle Course
- Set your course
- Give each contestant a chance to memorize the obstacle course
- Blindfold them and time their performance
- At random have someone remove all the obstacles while they are blindfolded and you are explaining the rules.

While they try to maneuver past the missing obstacles the crowd goes crazy with laughter.

Pole Sanding—

Divide group into man/woman couples, give each man a dowel about two feet long with a strip of paint about two inches from the top and about three inches long. Give the women a sheet of sandpaper. Instruct the men to hold the dowel between their legs from the back. On your mark the women are to sand off the spot of paint. Ready, set, go!

It's really funny when these couples are not really couples!

Mummify Your Partner—

Divide into teams of three or more, each team gets two rolls of toilet paper, the object is to mummify one of their teammates first. The team with the most complete coverage wins! Ready, set, go!

67.
Group Poker

This game is designed to keep people in your bar for longer periods of time. You'll need several decks of cards, depending on how many people come in, and a prize worth sticking around for.

Begin at a designated time by handing out a playing card to everyone at the bar. When someone new comes in, make sure they get a card. About three hours before closing, deal two cards to the bar (the flop). Tape them to the bar or somewhere where everyone can see them. Every half hour deal the bar another card until you have six cards showing and the card the customers hold makes the seventh card.

Best five cards wins!

TRY and get all the cards back but if you don't it really doesn't matter.

68.
Balloon Musical Chairs

This is another game that can be done any time, with very little supplies and should be done spontaneously whenever the mood starts getting a little stale.

Depending on how far apart people are sitting, you may be able to pull this off without anyone having to get up right away. Blow enough balloons for everyone except one person (get the customers to help).

The customers pass their balloons in the same direction as the music plays, when the music stops, whoever doesn't have a balloon is out! Remove a balloon and continue until there is only one person left! This game should raise the excitement level and change the mood considerably.

A great prize for the winner of this game is a complimentary drink!

69.
Local Cabbies

Local cab drivers are the bar owners best friend, do whatever you can to get these guys and gals name and address. Make sure they know what you have planned for your bar. They are constantly asked where to go by their customers, give them a stack of your two for one coupons, treat them like V.I.P.'s. Send them your calendar of events. Bars ands cabs go hand in hand, help each other out!

70.
Cheap Cigarettes

This promo is designed to get a good customer base day after day. Here's how it works.

You keep cigarettes behind your bar and sell them at or below your cost! I know it sounds crazy, but stay with me.

Advertise outside your bar on a marquee/mailer or wherever you can (check with your local and federal laws) that you sell cigarettes for $__ (price them at or slightly below your cost). In the fine print state, "With purchase, limit one pack per day."

By selling your cigarettes below cost, you are pretty much guaranteeing that your price is the lowest anyone is going to find. Smokers will notice this and appreciate it immediately. By making this offer good only good with purchase, you are insuring that the customer is not just going to stop in for cigarettes and leave. they have to purchase something. Even if they only purchase a soda, your profit margin on the soda will cover your loss on the cigarettes (even if they only stay for one drink), and you have accomplished the goal of getting someone new into your place. Now the chances that they will come back when they want a drink are greatly increased.

Take a little poll of your own. How many of your customers come in for just one drink and leave? But if they do that's fine too, because they are limited to one pack a day so chances are they will be back when they need another pack.

Funny thing about the bar business—When people are in your bar they attract more people. The real battle is getting them in the door.

71.
Fuzzy Bunny

This is a great promo that only takes a few minutes and creates a great new energy throughout the bar! You'll need a package of large marshmallows and a big bucket. Randomly grab four or five people from the bar and bring them in front of the group. Line them up and explain to them and to the crowd that you will start with the first in line, they have to grab a marshmallow, put it in their mouth (they cannot chew or swallow), and say "Fuzzy Bunny." The crowd will applaud if they think it was audible, or Boo if they think it was not. If they are boo-ed, they are eliminated If all the contestants make it to round two, they stuff another marshmallow in their mouth. By round 4 or 5, the laughter and silliness can get explosive. Literally! The rounds continue until there is only one bunny left. Make sure the bucket is nearby! First place wins a prize of your choice.

72.
Press Release

This is a very simple form of advertising.

Your neighborhood papers and magazines, radio shows and local news are always looking for human interest stories to fill empty space, dead time, etc. Spend a few hours with the phone book or on the internet collecting a master list of all your local media names and contact info, including their e-mail, fax number address and contact person. When talking to these folks ask whom you would send your human-interest press release to. This is the person or department that should be on your regular mailing/fax list.

When setting up your Fax or e-mail dedicate the top fifth of your page with the words

"PRESS RELEASE"

Follow this with your business information, name, address telephone number, directions, website, contact person, hours of operation, etc. Next, explain in detail your event(s) date and time, and complete description.

Keep in mind a scrambling editor will use your press release word for word to fill space come press time, so write it as you would like your potential customers to read it. Don't get discouraged if you don't see any reports of your press releases, just keep sending them in. Worst-case scenario is you will catch the attention of a local journalist and start seeing recommendations to your events through their columns.

73.
A Note to Barstaff

As you've probably gathered by now, the main thing on the small business owners mind is to create more income. If you are looking for a way to break into this business or just looking to make more money for yourself, make their goal your goal. Become the promoter. By accepting the "boss's" business goal as your primary job description, you have instantly elevated your position within the company. Your thought process will instantly change, creating a much more collaborative relationship than the everyday employee/employer relationship. Don't ask for a larger hourly wage for your involvement.

Instead, approach this from the small business owner's standpoint. Separate yourself from the mass of people that want more from your boss. instead offer your boss a raise! By offering your promotional services in exchange for a piece of the increased business, say 10% of the increase, how can he/she refuse?

Worst-case scenario the boss makes nothing, and it costs him/her nothing. Best-case scenario, you put some extra cash in your pocket and your value as an employee skyrockets! Your value to the company is only as much as you bring to the company. If you bring excuses and headaches, you will eventually be looking for a new gig. If you bring silver and gold, than you will be rewarded in silver and gold. Attitude is everything! Good Luck!

74.
Ding Dong The Witch is Dead!

One of our regular customers was a huge Wizard of Oz fan. She asked to have her birthday party at the bar, of course I said yes. She wanted to have a Wizard of Oz theme. She had all the decorations, and the movie. She wanted the movie playing in the background during the party. No problem. She had invitations printed up and the calls started coming in. Surprised by the type of calls we were getting, I had an outdoor banner made that read—

"Ding Dong the Witch is Dead!
Wizard of Oz Party
Sat Feb 18th 8pm"
then in very small print we added
"Happy Birthday Suzie!"

Saturday night was a great success! About half the people showed up in costume. Suzie commented that she knew only about 20 people at the party; there were well over 100 people throughout the night

Towards the end of the night we pulled down the outdoor banner and people throughout the bar signed it and we gave it to Suzie as a birthday card.

Based on the success of this party we started having Movie/ T.V. themed parties every month. I always let the customers suggestions determine the next party. We added a costume contest to create the right energy for the party. The costumes were the best part!!

75.
Ongoing Novel

In my home state, bars are required to keep a bar log behind the bar. It is a journal used to report any alcohol related incidents within the bar. I was always surprised at how many regular customers would know about the Log, and how many employees used it as their personal complaint diary. I required all my employees to write in it daily, just a little blurb about how their shift was, who came in etc.

One day I walked in and a group of about five or six regulars sat roaring in laughter. When I approached them I saw that they were reading our bar log. Then learned that during slow times, the day bartender would read excerpts from the log to the regulars. I realized that it read like a really bad soap opera. That's when I had the idea for the ongoing novel. I purchased another large bound journal, wrote "Ongoing Novel" on the cover, along with the name of the place and, "A not so true, true story." Then on the front page I wrote these instructions...

"This is an ongoing Novel. Feel free to write as often as you like, reading what has been written before you, adding to it, and leaving the next writer something to work with. Have fun and happy writing!"

Then I started the Novel...

"It was a cold blistery winter day. Don stumbled into the bar, alerting the bartender that it must be 3:47, as Don is never a minute early nor a minute late. His tired, aged, decrepit face showed the exhaustion of another hard day laboring in the rat infested city sewers. As he sat, dreaming about the frosty 16oz can of Beer that had been calling his name all day, he was rudely awakened by a loud blood curdling scream. Turning in his barstool, nothing could have prepared him for what he was about to see..."

Our bar novel lasted about 6 months and crossed over two journals! I noticed a lot of wives coming in to read and write in the journal. I had intended to have the book printed up and sell copies behind the bar, but that idea never happened.

Overall, this promo kind of rekindled a great energy and enthusiasm within the bar and introduced a lot of the daytime wives to our bar community.

76.
Block Party

This promo can be used any time you want to help raise funds.

We had a customer that was going through some unusually rough times and was faced with losing their home. Another customer told me of the problems she was facing and suggested starting a collection within the bar. The customer we were talking about was very well liked, and I new that many of our other customers would jump in to help.

That night I saw an old re-run of Good Times, where someone was going to lose their apartment and their friends and neighbors throw a party to raise some rent money. I proposed the same idea, and we organized a block party.

We made up a flyer announcing the party and why we were raising the money. We charged a $10 cover charge, and asked for people to bring a side dish, we left a big bucket for donations near the food line. I even found a band that volunteered to play for the party. I created a special drink called "The Man" it was served in a large water glass (to appear bigger) and we charged $3 more than normal. We held a 50/50 auction at the end of the night with half the proceeds going to the cause. Overall we were able to raise just over $1,000 to help out our customer. Everyone felt great about the party, and our guest of honor was greatly touched. WIN/WIN !

77.
The Dating Game

This promo started out as an attempt to get a singles crowd on Valentines Day. It soon became a regular promotion.

We sent out postcards and advertised in the local college paper for a singles Valentines Day party. I offered $1 ladies drinks. It's a well known fact that wherever the ladies are the men are sure to follow!

As the customers came through the door on event night they were given a name badge with a random number ranging from 1-300 preprinted on it. They were to put the name badge in plain view. Then when they saw someone they were interested in, they wrote a little note, folded it in half, put that person's badge number on the outside and posted it on the message board located between the bathrooms. As you went to the bathroom you checked the board for notes with your number. It was great!

The message board was our Community Bulletin Board cleared off for the night and located between the bathrooms.

A few well-placed flyers explaining the process and lots of scratch paper and pens and pencils are all you need! Cleaning up afterwards, reading some of the discarded notes was always my favorite part!

78.
Superbowl Widow

One bar I was involved in was extremely close to a large Sports Bar. Needless to say, whenever there was a sporting event, our sales suffered. Especially Superbowl! To try and combat impossible competition, we decided to market to the housewives. At first I thought of really playing the widow's theme with caskets, black veils, ect. Realizing this was too depressing I started asking for suggestions. Someone suggested a domestic wares party. We didn't have a better idea so we contacted a few reps until we found a Tupperware rep, pampered Chef rep and a Candle Light rep. They all agreed to host a party simultaneously in the bar. We provided a small assortment of appetizers and a variety of drink specials. As word got out, the buzz grew until event day. At the end of the Party, we were all very happy with the sales and began brainstorming how to maintain this following.

The reps all were very happy. They informed us that we were entitled to a bunch of free stuff for having the party. Which was great for future bar prizes.

THE END

Check out our website for new promotions!

www.promos2profits.com

Share your ideas with us!

I hope you have as much fun with these ideas as I have had over the years compiling them! Since the first drafts of this book were distributed, I have received several letters and e-mails from different operators with promo's they have used. I am in the process of compiling a second book of promo's Promo's 2 Profits 2. I invite you to share your ideas with us for the next book! Good Luck! & I hope to hear from you soon!!

—Aaron Wright

Get a free copy of *Promo's 2 Profits # 2*!

Do you have a promotion that has worked for you? When we publish it in our next book or website, we'll send you a free copy!

Send your promo idea to:

P.O. Box 2982

Clackamas, OR 97015

Or visit us online at:

www.promos2profits.com

Inspire your Staff!

Buy them each a copy of this book and
watch their creative ideas flow!

Buy 10 copies of Promo's to Profits for only $199.99!

One inspired promotion will more than cover the cost!

Buy 20 copies of Promo's to Profits for only $299.00

add $1 per book for shipping charges (Outside U.S. add $3 per book).

Send your check or money order to:

Promo's 2 Profits

Employee book order

P.O. Box 2982

Clackamas, Oregon 97015

or order online at **www.averagejoepublishing.com**

Aaron Wright has worked with small business owners from all over the US. He is an active Small Business Development Coach in his hometown of Portland, Oregon, where he resides with his wife and two children.

His online workshop BUILDING A PROFITABLE BUSINESS SYSTEM has enabled him to offer his proven business planning system to entrepreneurs worldwide. This twelve week program will provide you with not only a workable business system catered to your specific business, but will show you how to create a business system for all your future ventures! For more information on this course, visit

www.buildingaprofitablebusinesssystem.com

"The Science of Getting Rich"

Excerpt

....THERE is a thinking stuff from which all things are made, and which, in its original state, permeates, penetrates, and fills the interspaces of the universe.

A thought in this substance produces the thing that is imagined by thought.

Man can form things in his thought, and by impressing his thoughts upon formless substance can cause the thing he thinks about to be created.

In order to do this, man must pass from the competitive to the creative mind, otherwise he cannot be in harmony with the Formless intelligence, which is always creative and never competitive in spirit.

Man may come into full harmony with the Formless Substance by entertaining a lively and sincere gratitude for the blessings it bestows upon him. Gratitude unifies the mind of man with the intelligence of Substance, so that man's thoughts are received by the Formless. Man can remain upon the creative plane only by uniting himself with the Formless Intelligence through a deep and continuous feeling of gratitude

Man must form a clear and definite mental image of the things he wishes to have, to do, or to become, and he must hold this mental image in his thoughts, while being deeply grateful to the Supreme that all his desires are granted to him. The man who wishes to get rich must spend his leisure hours in contemplating his Vision, and in earnest thanksgiving that the reality is being given to him. Too much stress cannot be laid on the importance of frequent contemplation of the mental image, coupled with unwavering faith and devout gratitude. This is the process by which the impression is given to the Formless, and the creative forces set in motion.

The creative energy works through the established channels of natural growth, and of the industrial and social order. All that is included in his mental image will surely be brought to the man who follows the instructions given above, and whose faith does not waver. What he wants will come to him through the ways of established trade and commerce.

In order to come to his own when it shall come to him, man must be active, and this activity can only consist in more than filling his present place. He must keep in mind the Purpose to get rich through the realization of his mental image. And he must do, every day, all that can be done that day, taking care to do each act in a successful manner. He must give to every man a use value in excess of the cash value he receives, so that each transaction makes for more life, and he must so hold the Advancing thought that the impression of increase will be communicated to all with whom he comes in contact.

The men and women who practice the foregoing instructions will certainly get rich, and the riches they receive will be in exact proportion to the definiteness of their vision, the fixity of their purpose, the steadiness of their faith, and the depth of their gratitude...

—*Wallace Waddles*

Notes

Notes

Notes

Notes

Notes

Notes

Notes

Notes

Notes

Notes

Notes